E. McCier's Tasteful Thoughts

Featuring Fly Ty's Fruit Smoothies and Juices

Foreword

This book is proof that you never know exactly where this life may lead you. I honestly never gave it a thought to publish a cookbook, as I am not the greatest cook in the world myself, ironically, but luckily I was able to cross paths with a great person who also happens to be a great chef, Miss Erica McCier. I was in the process of publishing my ninth book when we had a conversation and I suggested that she print and publish her personal recipes in a cook book, and she said she would think on it. A few days later, she called me and said she was interested and she wanted me to be a part of it. Being that I make smoothies and fruit juices at home, I felt I could contribute to her book in a positive way so I decided to join her. I love educating my community anyway that I can and the foods we choose to eat are very important to maintaining good overall health. I hope we were able to help you choose a healthier lifestyle through the recipes that we came up with in this publication. Whether it is through the foods you consume or the juices you drink on a daily basis, all of it adds up to overall great health. Stay strong and focused in your travels. Train filthy, eat clean.

Peace....

Fly Ty Unchained

Edited by Fly Ty Unchained
ISBN: 978-1-312-43475-2

Acknowledgments

I would like to thank my children Gena, CJ and Brandon for giving me the blessing to step out and try new things in my life without judgment. For never giving up on mom even when she was not the easiest person to deal with. Thanks to my mother Elizabeth (Jean) McCier-Lomax for being my powerhouse, my strength and my backbone. You have been my biggest supporter in life and my career. My grandparents, the late Napolian and Molcy P. McCier. You taught me that we may be broke at times but never poor. As long as there was a roof over our heads, clothes on our backs, food on the table and hustle in our blood there were no worries. To the whole McCier clan. Lord knows I would need about 10 pages to list all of y'all. LOL. Every last one of you knows that you mean the world to me. My baby brother, James S. Lomax who has always been by my side holding my hand through all of the setbacks, hardships and heartaches. You always let your big sister think she was right even when she was wrong. LOL. I guess that is what little brothers are for right? My role model, Angela Lomax-Lee. We are so unstoppable cousin, there is nowhere for us to move but up from here. Special thanks to my sister-cousins, Joyce McCier-Rice, Audrea McCier-Klugh, Deborah McCier-Clinkscales, Ethel McCier-Atkinson, Sharon Williams-Dublin and Mildred D. Williams. I thank God so much for you women. Just like a true southern family, you took your little cousin under your wings and treated her as a little sister. Boy, we had our arguments, fistfights and throw downs but I could get no better love from a group of beautiful and intelligent queens.

Thanks to Bill and Molly Savitz, my first true culinary bosses and all of my Village Grill family. You guys have taught me that no matter how crazy this world gets, you just go crazy with it. LOL.. Thank you for allowing me to be a part of your family. Oh and Molly you still owe me a road trip. Thanks to Mayor Sarah Sherwood, my biggest cheerleader. You put my name out there chick and I could never thank you enough.

I would never leave out the world's best friend, Belinda Marshall. Girl thank you for just listening. You are the one who taught me that sometimes people don't need your advice, they just want you to listen. Through all of that moaning, groaning, complaining and crying over the years you never left me. You remained that true friend. That number one Ride or Die!!!! Forty years from now we'll still be reminiscing about the silly stuff that we did in middle school, the dumb stuff we did in high school, the foolish stuff we did in college and the crazy stuff we did as adults. LOL...

Special thanks to Mr. Tyrone Cooper aka Fly Ty Unchained. Never in my life would I have imagined doing a project like this. Thank you for that spark and that motivation. I never told you this but you are the one who has taught me how to stay hungry but remain humble. You my king are truly a righteous man and I could never repay for what you have done for me.

Be Blessed, Much Love and Thank You All,

Erica M. McCier

I would like to thank my sun Tyrone Cooper Jr for always being my inspiration in life to do greater things. As he gets older, I realize more and more the importance that a father plays in their suns lives, it's a beautiful thing to watch him grow and I am proud to say I'm his dad. I would also like to thank Erica M. McCier for putting her trust and faith in me in working on this project. I never thought I would be publishing a recipe cookbook but when you have friends such as Erica, anything is possible. I admire her drive and determination to succeed and advance in her field and in life. I look forward to the success of this book and I am also looking forward to ordering food from her establishment one day in the near future.

Peace...

Fly Ty Unchained

Cover Photo Provided By:

Keisha Quarles
Aim to Create
www.aimtocreate.com

Table of Contents:

Introduction

I grew up in the small southern town of Abbeville, SC where I still reside today with my three children Jergenia, Curtis Jr. and Brandon (Rayford). I come from an extremely large family who loves fellowship and eating. As an adolescent, I could hardly ever recall going to the grocery store to buy food because whatever we ate my grandparents either killed it or grew it. In a sense, we were living the organic lifestyle before it even became a fad. My grandparents largely influenced my passion for cooking, from my grandmother having biscuits, soups and stews on the stove every day, to my grandfather pressing the juice out of sugar canes making his own molasses.

After graduating from high school, I decided to major in Visual Arts. I earned my Bachelors and Master's degrees from Lander University (Greenwood, SC). Upon receiving my Master's I taught art for several years in the Abbeville County School District. During late 2007, I was diagnosed with Chronic Kidney Disease. Although I refuse to let this disease stagnate my life, I eventually ended up on life support for a period of two months in early 2009. This experience totally changed my life. I felt that everything that I had planned and worked so hard for had been taken away from me all because of this disease. After going through almost a year of depression I finally decided that, it was time for me to take back control of my life, not only for the sake of myself but for the sake of my children. I went from a stage in my life of being an active mother, teacher, Girl Scout leader, cheer leading coach and mentor to all of a sudden ending up on a dialysis machine for three days a week. Bored with my life I decided to go back to school, just to have something to do. I figured I like to cook so I would go to culinary school. At the time, I had no intentions of this becoming a career. I was just doing this to pass the time away until I could get a transplant and go back to teaching. However, God had different plans for me and my life began a total transformation. Everything that I desired before I became ill, I received afterward. My desires of being healed physically, mentally, financially and emotionally all came after the suffering of my kidney failure.

While in culinary school I began to have request to cater events for close friends and family, so in 2012, I started my own catering and personal chef business called Jean's Daughter Catering. My business went from preparing meals for families of four up to catering events for 300. The more I did this the more passionate I became about cooking. Cooking became my life. On February 10, 2013, I received a kidney transplant. I knew by now that I did not want to go back to teaching art and that being a chef was going to be my career. As of August 27, 2014, I graduated from culinary school and now claim the title as

Executive Chef of Bootleggers Taproom and Grill (Greenwood, SC). The most important thing that I have learned through my life experiences is that my plan was never the right plan for my life. Therefore, I'm learning to just live .... Just live, love life and not stress so much over what I want and accept what God has for me.

Staying Hungry but Remaining Humble,

Erica M. McCier

Chapter 1

Salads

Seared Chicken Breast over Mixed Greens and Granny Smith Apples with Honey Vinaigrette

Boneless chicken breast	two ea.
Olive oil	2 tablespoon
White wine vinegar	two fl oz.
White wine	two fl oz.
Canola oil	1/2 cup
Honey	four fl oz.
Baby mix lettuce (May substitute with other greens)	1 cup
Granny smith apple (Halved, cored and sliced thin)	one ea.
Walnut halves (toasted)	one/4 cup
Parmesan cheese (grated)	1/4 cup
Salt and ground black pepper	as needed

Directions:

1. Sear chicken in olive oil over medium heat. Remove from the heat and drain excessive oil.
2. Deglaze the pan with vinegar, white wine, oil and honey. Reduce by half and reserve for dressing.
3. Combine the greens, apples and walnuts in a bowl and toss with the dressing.
4. Place the greens in the center of a plate and top with chicken breast.
5. Garnish with Parmesan Cheese.

Roasted Pear Salad

Fresh pear (halved and cored)	4 ea.
Frisee	1 head
Red seedless grapes	as needed
Walnut pieces (roasted)	as needed
Blue cheese (crumbled)	2 oz.
Salt and ground black pepper	as needed
Olive oil	1/2 cup

Directions:

1. Preheat oven to 425 degrees
2. Roast the pears cut side up, until golden brown, remove from oven and allow to cool.
3. Cut the frisee into bundles and insert into the center of the pear. Arrange grapes, walnuts and blue cheese around the plate.
4. Drizzle with olive oil

Roasted Beet Salad with Walnuts and Goat Cheese

Red beets	5 ea.
Sherry vinegar	1 tablespoon
Walnut pieces	1 tablespoon
Shallot (minced)	1 tablespoon
Fresh chives (chopped)	1/2 tablespoon
Fresh parsley (chopped)	1/2 tablespoon
Watercress (cleaned and dry)	1 bunch
Baby mix lettuce	1/2 cup
Goat cheese	2 tablespoon

Directions:

1. Preheat oven to 425ºF
2. Roast beets until fork tender (approximately 30 minutes) remove from the oven and cool. Dice into large pieces or slice into thin pieces.
3. Combine the vinegar, oil, walnuts, shallots, chives and parsley and mix well. Season with salt and pepper
4. Arrange lettuce, beets and blue cheese onto the center of the plate and drizzle with dressing mixture.

Caesar Salad

Garlic	1 large clove
Egg, yolks pasteurized	2 yolks
Parmesan	1-2 oz.
Balsamic	1/4 cup
Lemon juice	1 oz.
Dijon mustard	1 tablespoon
Anchovies	0.5 oz.
Worcestershire sauce	1 teaspoon
Salt	1 teaspoon
Pepper	½ teaspoon
Olive oil	12 oz.
Croutons	2 oz.

Directions:

1. Crush the garlic in the bottom of the bowl until there are not lumps left.
2. Repeat with the anchovies.
3. Add the pasteurized egg yolks, mustard, vinegar, Worcestershire, and lemon juice.
4. Add the oil slowly to emulsify.
5. Add the croutons to the dressing.
6. Add the romaine and Parmesan cheese
7. Toss lightly to dress.

Lobster Roll

Lobster meat	3/4 lb.
Mayonnaise	4 oz.
Celery (stalk with leaves, finely chopped)	1 ea.
Green onion (chopped)	1 ea.
Fresh parsley (chopped)	1 tablespoon
Ground black pepper	to taste
Salt	to taste
Soft rolls (oblong)	4 ea.
Butter (melted, for brushing)	1 oz.

Directions:

1. Remove the meat from the lobsters, chopping any large chunks into bite-size pieces. In a bowl, combine the lobster meat, mayonnaise, lemon juice, celery, parsley, green onion and salt and pepper to taste.
2. Place lobster salad in refrigerator for 5 to 10 minutes. This allows the salad to absorb the flavorings.
3. Brush cut sides of the rolls with melted butter and fills with the lobster salad

Chapter 2

Sandwiches

Grilled BBQ Portabella Mushroom Sandwich on Focaccia

Focaccia (cut into 6-in. squares)	3 ea.
Portabella mushrooms	3 ea.
Barbecue Sauce	1 fl oz.
Red bell pepper (roasted, peeled, julienne)	1 ea.
Fresh basil	15 leaves
Soy cheese (or other vegetarian cheese, crumbled)	3 tablespoon

Directions:

1. Slice the focaccia squares horizontally and toast.
2. Brush the mushrooms with the Barbecue Sauce and grill until hot and tender.
3. To assemble each sandwich, place one mushroom on the bottom of a focaccia square and top with one-sixth of the bell pepper strips, five basil leaves and 1 tablespoon of cheese. Top with the remaining focaccia cut in half and serve.

Grilled Vegetable Sandwich

Eggplant (cut into 1/4 inch thick slices)	1/2 ea.
Salt	1/2 teaspoon
Zucchini (cut into 1/4 inch thick slices)	1/2 ea.
Yellow squash (cut into 1/4 inch thick slices)	1/2 ea.
Red onion	1/2 ea.
Olive oil	1 1/2 fl oz.
Garlic (minced)	1 tablespoon
Herbs de Provence	1/2 teaspoon
Ground black pepper	as needed
Multigrain sandwich rolls	3 ea.
Bourse cheese	2 oz.
Green leaf lettuce	3 leaves
Red bell pepper (roasted, cut into strips)	3 oz.

Directions:

1. Sprinkle the eggplant with salt and set aside in a colander for 10 minutes.
2. Dry the sliced zucchini, squash and eggplant with paper towels. Place them on a sheet pan with the onion slices. Brush the vegetables with the oil and sprinkle with the garlic and herbs de Provence. Season with more salt and pepper.
3. Place the sliced vegetables on a hot grill without crowding. Grill until lightly charred and done, approximately 4 to 5 minutes on each side. (The vegetables may be prepared ahead of serving. Refrigerate until needed.)
4. Split each roll in half. Spread the herb-garlic cheese generously on the top half of each roll. Arrange one-sixth of the lettuce, onion, bell peppers, squash and eggplant in layers on each roll. Place the tops on the sandwiches and serve immediately.

Black Bean Vegetable Slider with Roasted Garlic and Herb Spread

Black Bean Vegetable Cake	
Canned black beans	7 oz.
Onion	¼ cup
Green bell pepper	¼ cup
Ground cumin	½ teaspoon
Chili powder	1 teaspoon
Salt	½ teaspoon
Dried bread crumbs	½ cup
Vegetable spray	as needed
Soft rolls (for sliders)	8 ea.

Directions:

1. Drain and rinse beans in cold water.
2. Place all the ingredients into the mixer with the paddle attachment. Mix on low until beans are broken and binding together.
3. Portion and Place on a parchment lined sheet pan.
4. Spray the tops of the cakes with pan spray to prevent them from drying out.
5. Bake in a 350°F oven until internal temperature reaches 165°F.
6. Top with cheese and continue to cook until cheese is melted.
7. Assemble sliders on soft rolls with lettuce, tomato, cheese and desired condiments

Grouper Sandwich with Lemon Rémoulade

Olive oil	1 fl oz.
Grouper fillet	6 ea.
Salt	to taste
Ground black pepper	to taste
Lemon Rémoulade	3 fl oz.
Kaiser rolls (sliced, toasted)	6 ea.
Baby mix lettuce	3 cups
Fresh tomatoes	6 slices

Directions:

1. Heat the oil in a large sauté pan. Season the grouper fillets with salt and pepper and then sauté the fish until golden brown and cooked through.
2. To assemble each sandwich, spread 1/2 fluid ounce of Lemon Rémoulade on the bottom half of the roll, then top with 1/2 cup mixed greens, one tomato slice and one cooked fish fillet. Cover with the remaining half of the roll and serve.

Lemon Rémoulade

Mayonnaise	1/4 cup
Green onion (chopped fine)	1 teaspoon
Fresh parsley (chopped)	1 teaspoon
Lemon Juice (fresh)	1 teaspoon
Salt	to taste
Ground black pepper	to taste
Worcestershire sauce	to taste
Tabasco sauce	to taste
Garlic (minced)	1 clove

Directions

1. Mix all the ingredients together until thoroughly blended.

Southwestern Grilled Chicken Wrap

Boneless skinless chicken breast	12 oz.
Salt	to taste
Ground black pepper	to taste
Avocado (Haas)	6 oz.
Red bell pepper	6 oz.
Red onion	6 oz.
Fresh tomatoes	4 oz.
Flour tortilla (12 in.)	3 ea.
Black Bean Spread	12 oz.
Pitted black olives (sliced)	1 1/2 oz.
Fresh cilantro (chopped)	1/2 bunch
Yellow cheddar cheese (grated)	6 oz.
Jalapeno Chile pepper (minced)	1/2 ea.
Sour cream (or fresh salsa)	as needed

Directions:

1. Season the chicken breast with salt and pepper and grill or broil until done. Cool and cut into strips.
2. Peel the avocados and cut each into 12 slices. Clean the bell peppers and cut into 1/4- inch strips. Slice the onion thinly. Dice the tomatoes.
3. To make each sandwich, place one tortilla on a cutting board and spread with approximately 4 ounces Black Bean Spread.
4. Sprinkle half of the bell peppers, onion, tomatoes, olives, cilantro, cheese and jalapenos over the bean spread.
5. Top with half of the chicken and three slices of avocado. Drizzle each wrap with salsa or sour cream, if desired.
6. Roll the tortilla around the ingredients tightly enough so that the sandwich will hold its shape.

Turkey Burgers

Fresh ginger (minced)	1 teaspoon
Garlic (minced)	1/2 teaspoon
Sesame oil	1/2 teaspoon
Medium mushrooms (chopped)	2 oz.
Green onion (chopped fine)	1/2 ea.
Ground turkey	10 oz.
Salt	1/4 teaspoon
Ground black pepper	1/8 teaspoon

Glaze	
Soy sauce	2 teaspoon
Sesame oil	1 teaspoon
Fresh ginger (minced)	1/4 teaspoon
Garlic (chopped)	1/2 teaspoon
Pita bread or flat breads	2 ea.
Sesame seeds	2 teaspoon
Iceberg lettuce	as needed
Fresh tomatoes	as needed

Directions:

1. Sauté the ginger and garlic in the sesame oil for 1 minute. Add the mushrooms and onion and sauté approximately 1 minute longer. Do not fully cook the mushrooms; allow them to retain most of their liquid in order to add moisture to the finished burgers.
2. Remove the mushroom mixture from the heat, spread on a sheet pan and refrigerate until cold.
3. Combine the cold mushroom mixture with the ground turkey, salt and pepper and mix well. Form the mixture into four patties.
4. Stir the glaze ingredients together.
5. Oil the grate of a hot grill. Brush the burgers with the glaze and grill to an internal temperature of 165°F basting occasionally with the glaze.
6. Serve each burger open-faced on toasted warm flat bread. Sprinkle with sesame seeds and serve accompanied by lettuce leaves, tomato slices or other garnishes as desired.

Turkey and Havarti Cuban sandwich with Cranberry Chutney

Sub rolls	4 each
Smoked turkey	1 lbs.
Havarti cheese	as needed
Mayo	as needed

Cranberry chutney	
Onion, diced	1 each
Cranberries, dried	2 cups
Apple juice	3 cups
Mustard seeds, cracked	1 tablespoon

Directions:

1. This is a pressed type of sandwich similar to a grilled cheese or Panini; this is to be made on the griddle with a pan on top.
2. Combine the onions, cranberries, apple juice, and mustard seed together in a pot, cook until it has reduced to proper consistency.
3. Put the mayo on each half of bread.
4. Place the chutney on the top half of the bread.
5. Place the Havarti on the top of the bread.
6. Place the turkey on the bottom slice.
7. Assemble.
8. If not using a Panini press, place on the griddle with butter and place a heavy pan/pot on top to press the sandwich.
9. Flip on the side to brown.
10. Portion and serve.

Monte Cristo Sandwiches

White bread	4 Slices
Egg	1 each
Milk	2 oz.
Salt	Pinch
Butter	as needed
Turkey breast, thinly sliced	as needed
Swiss cheese	4 slices
Confectioners' sugar	as garnish
Jelly or jam	as condiment

Directions:

1. Whisk the salt, egg, and milk together.
2. Dip the bread into the egg batter.
3. Using the butter, cook on the griddle like French toast.
4. Flip the bread and place a slice of cheese on each piece.
5. Place the turkey on the other half.
6. Combine the turkey and ham halves to finish the sandwiches.
7. Garnish with confectioner's sugar and serve a heated jam as a side condiment.

Chapter 3

Seafood

Teriyaki Salmon with Pineapple Papaya Salsa

Marinade	
Soy sauce	4 fl oz.
Garlic (crushed)	1/2 teaspoon
Fresh ginger (minced)	1/2 teaspoon
Dark brown sugar	1 oz.
Sake	2 fl oz.
Salmon	(4 oz.) 2 ea.
Vegetable oil	1 fl oz.

Directions:

1. To make the marinade, combine the soy sauce, garlic, ginger, brown sugar and sake.
2. Marinate the salmon in the marinade for 15 minutes.
3. Remove the salmon from the marinade and pat dry. Brush the tranches with oil and broil or grill until done.
4. Serve the salmon on a bed of warmed Pineapple Papaya Salsa.

Pineapple Papaya Salsa

Pineapple	4 oz.
Fresh papaya	2 oz.
Green onion (sliced)	3/4 ea.
Fresh cilantro (chopped)	1/4 bunch
Jalapeno Chile pepper (seeded, minced)	1/4 ea.
Lemon Juice (fresh)	1 1/4 teaspoon
Garlic (chopped)	1/4 teaspoon
Salt	1/4 teaspoon

Directions:

1. Core and dice the tomatoes.
2. Peel and dice the pineapple.
3. Peel, seed and dice the papaya.
4. Combine all the ingredients and chill well.

Broiled Tilapia or Flounder

Tilapia or Flounder	
Salt and pepper	To Taste
Paprika	to Taste
Olive oil	as needed

Directions:

1. Preheat oven to 350 degrees.
2. Place fish on a sheet pan.
3. Drizzle olive oil on both sides of the fish.
4. Season with salt, pepper and paprika on both sides
5. Place in oven and cook for 10-15 minutes or until the fish is white and flaky.

Shrimp and Corn Sauté

16-20 CT shrimp (peeled, deveined and tails removed)	6 oz.
Unsalted butter	1 oz.
Red bell pepper (small dice)	1 oz.
Green bell pepper (small dice)	1 oz.
Fresh corn (kernels)	6 oz.
Heavy cream	2 fl oz.
Ground black pepper	to taste
Salt	to taste

Directions:

1. Sauté the shrimp in 1 ounce (30 grams) of the butter until tender. Remove the shrimp and set aside. Sauté the bell peppers
2. in the remaining butter until tender.
3. Add the corn and the cream and sauté until hot.
4. Return the shrimp to the pan and cook until all ingredients are hot. Adjust the seasonings with salt and pepper.

Shrimp Scampi

Garlic (roasted and minced)	2 cloves
Salt and pepper	To Taste
Shrimp	2 lbs.
Butter	2 tablespoon
Lemon Juice	As Needed
Heavy cream	As Needed
White wine	1 oz.

Directions:

1. Roast garlic and mince.
2. Season the shrimp with salt and pepper
3. Sauté shrimp with garlic and remove from pan.
4. Deglaze pan with white wine and lemon juice.
5. Add cream and reduce sauce by half.
6. Turn heat off.
7. Flake in the butter.
8. Serve over Pasta

Crab Cakes

Lump crab	2 ½ lb.
Eggs	2 ea.
Mayonnaise	¼ cup
Dijon mustard	2 tablespoon
Fresh Italian parsley (chopped)	as needed
Louisiana hot sauce	1 tablespoon
Panko bread crumbs	½ cups

Directions:

1. Heat oven to 375 degrees
2. Pick the crab and set aside.
3. Mix the mayo, mustard, eggs, parsley, and hot sauce and combine with the crab.
4. Fold together and mix well, slowly add the breadcrumbs to bind together
5. Portion into 1 oz. crab cakes.
6. Place in oven on a sheet pan and cook for approximately 10-15 minutes or until golden brown.

Note: Crab cakes can also be fried in a shallow amount of oil.

Stuffed Crab Wontons with Apricot Sauce

Cream cheese	8 oz.
Crab meat	8 oz.
Garlic (minced)	1 teaspoon
Green onions (sliced)	1 oz.
Salt and pepper	to taste
Worcestershire sauce	to taste
Sesame oil	to taste
Wonton wraps	24
Apricot sauce	as needed

Directions:

1. Place cream cheese in a bowl of a mixer and mix until soft.
2. Place the crabmeat, garlic and green onions. Season with salt and pepper, Worcestershire sauce and sesame oil.
3. Place wonton wraps on work surface, Brush the edges with water. Place t tablespoon of the mixture in the center of each wrap. Fold the wonton skin in half to form a triangle and seal the edges.
4. Deep fry the wontons until golden brown. Remove and drain oil.

Apricot Sauce

Apricot preserves	8 oz.
Fresh ginger, grated	1 tablespoon
Dry mustard	1 teaspoon
Rice wine vinegar	½ fl. Oz

Directions:

1. Combine all ingredients and heat until preserves melt and the flavors blend.

Shrimp with Goat Cheese Grits

Water	4 cups
Salt and pepper	to taste
Stone-ground grits	1 cup
Butter	3 tablespoons
Goat cheese	2 cup
Shrimp, peeled and deveined	1 pound
Heavy cream	as needed
Lemon juice	4 teaspoons
Chopped parsley	2 tablespoons
Thinly sliced scallions	1 cup
Garlic, minced	1 clove

Directions:

1. Bring water to a boil. Add salt and pepper. Add grits and cook until water is absorbed, about 20 to 25 minutes. Remove from heat and stir in butter and cheese.
2. Rinse shrimp and pat dry. Cook until shrimp turn pink. Add lemon juice, cream, parsley, scallions and garlic. Sauté for 3 minutes.
3. Spoon grits into a serving bowl. Add shrimp mixture and mix well. Serve immediately.

Pistachio Crusted Round Fish (Salmon)

Salmon	5 lbs. .
Salt and pepper	to taste
Goat Cheese	8 oz.
Tarragon, dry	¼ oz.
Pistachio	1 lb.

Directions:

1. Soften the goat cheese by mixing it by hand or in a mixer.
2. Grind the pistachios in a food processor, pulse this. If you grind to much the pistachio oil will start to come out and the mixture will be wet and crumbly.
3. Add the tarragon to the pistachio.
4. Portion the salmon into 4 oz. pieces.
5. Season the salmon with salt and pepper.
6. spread a thin layer of the goat cheese onto the fish (like putting mayo on a sandwich).
7. Blot the goat cheese side of the salmon in the pistachio tarragon mixture. And place on a pan.
8. Bake the salmon in a 350° oven for about 8-10 minutes ***being careful that the salmon does not OVERCOOK***

Macadamia Nut-Crusted Flounder with Red Onion, Tomato and Balsamic Salsa

Whole macadamia nuts	2 oz.
All-purpose flour	4 oz.
Flounder fillet (2 fillets, approx. 8 oz. each)	1 lb.
Salt	to taste
Ground black pepper	to taste
Eggs (slightly beaten)	1 ea.
Olive oil	as needed
Tomato and Balsamic Salsa Red Onion	1/2 pt.

Directions:

1. Place the nuts on a half-sheet pan and toast them lightly in the oven. Combine the toasted nuts with 2 ounces of the flour in a food processor. Process until the nuts are chopped finely, but not pulverized.
2. Season the fillets with salt and pepper and then bread them using the remaining flour and egg, the nut-flour mixture is the final coating.
3. Heat a frying pan and add a thin film of oil. Place the breaded fillets in the oil, leaving some space between each fillet so that they will cook properly.
4. Sauté the fillets until they are a deep golden brown and crusty, then turn them over and cook until the fish is medium rare to medium. Remove the fillets from the pan. Residual heat will complete the cooking.
5. Spoon some of the Red Onion, Tomato and Balsamic Salsa onto a serving platter and place the fillets on top of the salsa.

Red Onion, Tomato and Balsamic Salsa

Fresh tomatoes (seeded, small diced)	2 1/2 ea.
Red onion (sliced)	1 ea.
Garlic clove (minced)	1 1/2 ea.
Fresh cilantro (chopped)	1/4 bunch
Jalapeno Chile pepper (chopped fine)	1 1/2 ea.
Balsamic vinegar	2 fl oz.
Salt to taste	
Ground black pepper to taste	

Directions:

1. Combine all ingredients and gently toss. Adjust seasonings and refrigerate.

Chapter 4

Vegetables, Rice and Pasta

Asparagus in Pecan Butter

Asparagus	1 bunch
Unsalted butter	2 tablespoon
Pecans, Chopped	½ cup
Salt and pepper	to taste

Directions:

1. Trim and peel the asparagus to promote even cooking.
2. Boil the asparagus in salted water until tender, approximately 5 minutes.
3. Shock in ice bath.
4. Heat the butter in a sauté pan until it turns nutty brown.
5. Add the pecans and toss to brown them.
6. Add the asparagus and toss to reheat and blend flavors.
7. Adjust the seasonings and serve.

Curried Cauliflower

Canola Oil	¼ cup
Mustard Seed, Crushed	1 tablespoon
Yellow Curry Powder	1 tablespoon
Red Onion, Sliced	1 each
Cauliflower	2 heads
Sugar	¼ cup
Coconut Milk	1 can (12 oz.)
Salt and pepper	to taste

Directions:

1. Heat the canola oil.
2. Toast the mustard seed and curry powder.
3. Add the red onion and sauté until tender.
4. Add the sugar and coconut milk to the onion mixture and reduce by half.
5. Add the cauliflower to the mixture and cover.
6. Cook until tender. Adjust seasonings.

Ratatouille

Onion (medium dice)	3 oz.
Garlic (chopped)	3/4 teaspoon
Olive oil	1 oz.
Green bell pepper (medium dice)	1 1/2 oz.
Red bell pepper (medium dice)	1 1/2 oz.
Eggplant (medium dice)	3 oz.
Zucchini (medium dice)	2 oz.
Tomato (peeled and remove seeds)	6 oz.
Fresh basil (chiffonade)	1/4 oz.
Salt	1/4 oz.
Ground black pepper	to taste

Directions:

1. Sauté the onion and garlic in the oil.
2. Add the bell peppers, eggplant and zucchini and sauté until tender, approximately 10 minutes.
3. Add the tomato, basil and seasonings. Sauté for 5 minutes. Adjust the seasonings.

Collard Greens

Thick Cut Bacon or Turkey Bacon	8 oz.
Crushed red pepper	1/4 tsp
Water	as needed
Collard greens	2 lb.
Green onion (small dice)	1 ea.
Light brown sugar	1 tablespoon
Cider vinegar	1 fl oz.
Salt	to taste
Ground black pepper	to taste

Directions:

1. In a medium saucepot, combine the bacon and Chile flakes. Cover with 1 inch water, bring to a
Boil, reduce to a simmer and cook until the hocks are tender, approximately 1 hour. Remove, the hocks from the pot,
Reserving the cooking liquid, which is known as pot liquor?
2. Wash, trim and cut the collard greens. Add them to the pot liquor and simmer until tender, approximately 45 minutes to 1 hour.
3. Add the green onions, sugar and vinegar to the greens. Bring to a simmer and reduce the liquid until it coats the collard
Greens. Season to taste with salt and pepper.

Braised Red Cabbage with Apples and Red Wine

Red Cabbage	lbs.
Canola Oil	2 oz.
Onions, Medium Dice	2 oz.
Salt	to Taste
Pepper	to Taste
Red Wine	4 oz.
White Stock (Chicken)	5 oz.
Cinnamon Sticks	½ each
Apples, Granny Smith	1 each

Cored and Diced - ***Note: Toss with the Cider Vinegar to Keep From Oxidizing***

Brown Sugar	1 oz.
Cider Vinegar	3 oz.

Directions:

1. Shred the cabbage.
2. Add the onions and sweat in the oil until tender.
3. Add the cabbage and sauté for 5 minutes.
4. Season with salt and pepper.
5. Add the wine, stock and cinnamon sticks.
6. Cover and braise until the cabbage is almost tender, approximately 20-30 minutes.
7. Add the apples, brown sugar and vinegar and mix well.
8. Cover and braise until the apples are tender, approximately 5 minutes.
9. Taste to check seasoning, and adjust salt and pepper.

Stir Fried Asparagus with Shitake Mushrooms

Asparagus	lb.
Shitake mushrooms	Oz
Vegetable oil	1 tablespoon
Sesame oil	1 tablespoon
Shallots (thinly sliced)	3 oz.
Garlic (minced)	2 teaspoon
Oyster sauce	4 fl. Oz
Sesame seeds (garnish)	as needed

Directions:

1. Slice asparagus on a bias into 2-inch pieces
2. Clean mushrooms and remove stems. Cut mushroom caps into ½-inch slices.
3. Heat oil in a wok or sauté pan.
4. Add shallots and garlic, stir-frying for 30 seconds.
5. Add asparagus, sauté for 1 minute and then add mushrooms sautéing for another minute.
6. Add oyster sauce and garnish with sesame seeds

Roasted Butternut Squash

Butternut squash (medium dice)	1 lb.
Unsalted butter	3 oz.
Salt and pepper	to taste
Cinnamon	¼ teaspoon
Cardamom (ground)	1/8 teaspoon
Brown sugar	2 tablespoon

Directions:

1. Place squash in a buttered pan. Season with salt, pepper, cinnamon, cardamom and sugar.
2. Drizzle melted butter over top of the squash and bake uncovered in a 350º oven until tender, approximately 45-50 minutes

Roasted Vegetables

Butternut Squash (cubed)	1 each
Red Bell Pepper (large dice)	2 each
Sweet Potato (cubed)	1 each
Yukon Gold Potatoes (cubed)	3 each
Red Onion (quartered)	1 each
Fresh Thyme (chopped)	1 tablespoon
Fresh Rosemary (chopped)	2 tablespoon
Olive Oil	¼ cup
Balsamic Vinegar	2 tablespoon
Salt and Pepper	To Taste

Directions:

1. Preheat oven to 475ºF…
2. In a large bowl, combine the squash, red bell peppers, sweet potato, and Yukon Gold potatoes. Separate the red onion quarters into pieces, and add them to the mixture.
3. In a small bowl, stir together thyme, rosemary, olive oil, vinegar, salt, and pepper. Toss with vegetables until they are coated. Spread evenly on a large roasting pan.
4. Roast for 35 to 40 minutes in the preheated oven, stirring every 10 minutes, or until vegetables are cooked through and browned.

Creamy Mushroom and Broccoli Casserole

Butter	3 tablespoons plus extra for casserole dish
All-purpose flour	2 tablespoons
Mushrooms, sliced	1/2 pound
Onions, chopped	1/4 cup
Garlic, finely chopped	2 cloves
Garlic powder	1/2 teaspoon
Cayenne pepper	1/2 teaspoon
Heavy cream	cups
Chicken stock	1/2 cup
Frozen chopped broccoli, thawed and drained	1 (10-ounce) box
Cheddar-Monterey blend (Gueyer)	2 cups shredded
Cooked rice	3 cups
Salt and pepper	To Taste

Directions:

1. Preheat oven to 425 degrees. Butter casserole dish. In a large pot, melt 3 tablespoons butter and flour over medium heat until golden in color to make a quick roux. The roux should resemble the color of peanut butter.
2. Add mushrooms, onion, garlic, garlic powder, and cayenne pepper, heavy cream and chicken stock.
3. Add broccoli, 1 cup of the cheese and rice. Season with salt and pepper, to taste.
4. Pour into buttered dish and top with remaining shredded Cheddar.
5. Bake until cheese is melted and golden, about 20 minutes. (Optional, Add toasted breadcrumbs on top for a crunchy texture)

Baked Beans (Boston-Style)

Great northern beans (soaked)	½ lb.
Onion (small dice)	2 oz.
Anaheim Chile pepper (small dice)	1 oz.
Molasses	2 oz.
Dark brown sugar	2 oz.
Ketchup	4 oz.
Brown mustard seed	1 tablespoon
Cider vinegar	1 tablespoon
Worcestershire sauce	1 tablespoon
Tabasco sauce	to taste
Salt	to taste
Ground black pepper	to taste

Directions:

1. Simmer the beans in water until almost tender, approximately 45 minutes. Drain well.
2. Combine the remaining ingredients, blending well.
3. Add the sauce to the beans, tossing to coat thoroughly. Adjust the seasonings.
4. Place the beans in a hotel pan or a 2-quart (2-liter) baking dish. Cover and bake in a 350°F oven until the beans are completely tender, approximately 30 to 40 minutes.

Mashed Potatoes

Russet potato	2 lb. 8 oz.
Salt	1 1/2 tsp
Butter (melted & hot)	2 oz.
Milk (hot)	4 fl oz.
Salt	1 tsp
Ground white pepper	1/8 tsp

Directions:

1. Wash and peel the potatoes. Cut each potato into four to six uniform-sized pieces.
2. Place the potatoes in a pot, cover them with water and add 1-tablespoon (15 milliliters) salt to the water. Bring the water To a boil, reduce to a simmer and cook until the potatoes are tender. Do not overcook the potatoes.
3. When the potatoes are cooked, drain them well in a colander. The potatoes must be very dry. Transfer them to the bowl Of an electric mixer. Using the whip attachment, whip the potatoes for 30 to 45 seconds. Scrape the sides and bottom of the Bowl and whip for another 15 seconds or until the potatoes are smooth and free of lumps. The potatoes must be smooth Before adding any liquids or they will remain lumpy.
4. Add the butter, milk and seasonings. Whip on low speed to incorporate all of the ingredients. Scrape the sides and Bottom of the bowl and whip again for several seconds. Adjust consistency and seasoning.

VARIATIONS:

Garlic Mashed Potatoes

Sweat 1-ounce (30 grams) chopped garlic in the melted butter for 5 to 10 minutes without browning. Strain the butter if desired. Add the hot garlic butter in place of the melted butter in the recipe.

Herbal Rice

Unsalted Butter	2 oz.
Onion, Chopped Fine	2 oz.
Garlic Clove (minced)	1 each
Bay Leaf	2 each
Long-Grain Rice	2 cups
Water	4 cups
Salt	to Taste
Herb of Choice	

Directions:

1. Heat the oil and olive oil in a heavy saucepot with metal handles.
2. Add the onion and bay leaf and sauté until tender, but not brown. Add garlic after this process to avoid burning
3. Add the rice and stir to coat completely with the hot butter. Do not allow the rice to brown.
4. Pour in the water and season with salt.
5. Cover the pot tightly and place it in a 350°F oven. Bake for 18-20 minutes, until the liquid is absorbed and the rice is fluffy and tender.
6. Remove bay leaf and fluff the rice with a fork.

Brown Rice

Water	1 pt.
Salt	1/2 tsp
Brown rice	8 oz.

Directions:

1. Bring the water and salt to a boil in a heavy saucepan. Slowly add the rice.
2. Cover the pan and reduce the heat so that the liquid simmers gently. Cook until the rice is tender and the water is absorbed, approximately 15 to 20 minutes.
3. Remove from the heat and transfer to a hotel pan. Do not cover. Allow any excess moisture to evaporate for approximately 5 minutes. Fluff the rice and serve, or refrigerate for use in another recipe

Rice Pilaf/Spanish Rice

Clarified Butter	1/2 fl oz.
Olive oil	1/2 fl oz.
Onion (fine dice)	1 oz.
Dried bay leaves	1/2 ea.
Long grain rice	8 oz.
Chicken Stock (boiling)	16 fl oz.
Salt	to taste

Directions:

1. Heat the butter and oil in a heavy saucepot.
2. 2. Add the onion and bay leaf and sauté until the onion is tender, but not brown.
3. 3. Add the rice and stir to coat it completely with the hot fat. Do not allow the rice to brown.
4. 4. Pour in the boiling stock and season with salt.
5. 5. Cover the pot tightly and place it in a 350 degrees oven. Bake until the liquid is absorbed and the rice is fluffy and tender,
6. Approximately 18 to 20 minutes.
7. 6. Transfer the cooked rice to a hotel pan and fluff the rice with a fork. Remove the bay leaf and keep the rice hot for service.

VARIATION:

Spanish rice

Add three chopped garlic cloves and 1-tablespoon pure ground chili powder with the diced onion. In Step 3, sauté the rice until it browns slightly. In place of the Chicken stock, use half-chicken stock and half chopped canned tomatoes with juice. Add 1 tablespoon chopped cilantro when adding the liquids

Risotto Milanese

Unsalted butter	2 oz.
Onions minced	3 oz.
Arborio Rice	2 cups
Chicken stock	6 cups
Saffron threads, crushed	½ teaspoon
Dry white wine	4 oz.
Unsalted butter	2 oz.
Parmesan, grated	2 oz.

Directions:

1. Bring the chicken stock to a simmer and add the saffron and season with salt.
2. Heat the butter (2 oz.) in a large, heavy saucepan.
3. Add the onion and sauté without browning until translucent.
4. Add the rice to the onion and butter.
5. Stir well to coat the grains with butter but do not allow the rice to brown.
6. Add the wine and stir until it is completely absorbed.
7. Add the simmering stock, 2 ounces at a time, stirring frequently.
8. Wait until the stock is absorbed before adding the next 2-ounce portion.
9. After approximately 18-20 minutes, all the stock should be incorporated and the rice should be tender.
10. Remove from the heat and stir in the grated cheese and whole butter (2 oz.).
11. Serve immediately.

Note: Be careful not to over stir and break up starch.

Fettuccine Alfredo

Fettuccine	8 oz.
Unsalted butter	2 oz.
Heavy cream	12 fl. Oz
Parmesan cheese	2 oz.
Salt and pepper	to taste

Directions:

1. Boil pasta in salted water. Cook al dente (slightly undercooked) and drain.
2. To make sauce combine butter, heavy cream and cheese. Bring to a boil and reduce heat to a simmer.
3. Add pasta to sauce and simmer until sauce thickens.
4. Add cooked protein and adjust seasonings.

Variations

Chicken Alfredo-season chicken breast (boneless) with salt and pepper. Sauté until golden brown on each side. Continue cooking in a 350-degree oven until done or until internal temperature reaches 160 degrees.

Shrimp Alfredo- Season and sauté lbs. Of peeled and deveined shrimp. Substitute for step

Baked Ziti with Fresh Tomato Sauce

Eggs	3/4 ea.
Ricotta cheese	8 oz.
Fresh thyme (chopped)	3/4 teaspoon
Fresh oregano (chopped)	3/4 teaspoon
Fresh basil (chopped)	3/4 teaspoon
Salt	to taste
Ground black pepper	to taste
Turkey sausage links	10 oz.
Ziti pasta (cooked, refreshed, and drained)	12 oz.
Parmesan cheese (grated)	1 oz.
Fresh Tomato Sauce for Pasta	16 fl oz.
Mozzarella cheese (shredded)	4 oz.

Directions:

1. Combine the eggs, ricotta, thyme, oregano, basil, salt and pepper. Mix well and refrigerate.
2. Place the sausage links in a 2-inch- (5-centimeter-) deep full-size hotel pan; cook in a 350°F oven for 20 minutes. Remove and drain the sausage. Slice the links into rounds and reserve.
3. Pour off the sausage fat, then place the ziti in the hotel pan. Top with an even coating of the cheese mixture, sausage
Slices and Parmesan.
4. Pour the Fresh Tomato Sauce for Pasta over the top layer and stir slightly to distribute the sauce.
5. Bake at 375°F for 1 hour. Sprinkle the mozzarella evenly over the pasta and return to the oven for 10 minutes.
Serve.

Tomato Sauce

Mirepoix	
Onion	6 oz.
Carrot	3 oz.
Celery	3 oz.
Sachet (place herbs in cheesecloth, tie end tightly to seal)	
Dried whole thyme	1/2 tsp
Dried bay leaves	1 1/2 ea.
Garlic clove	1 1/2 ea.
Fresh parsley (stems only)	5 sprigs
Fresh tomatoes (or canned)	1 qtr. 16 fl oz.
Tomato purees	1 qtr.
Whole black pepper (crushed)	1/4 tsp
Salt	3/4 oz.
Granulated sugar	1/2 oz.

Directions:

1. Add the mirepoix and sauté, but do not brown.
2. Add the tomatoes, tomato puree, sachet, salt and sugar.
3. Simmer slowly for 1 to 2 hours or until the desired consistency has been reached.

Chapter 5

Poultry

Poached Breast of Chicken with Tarragon Sauce

Boneless skinless chicken breast	2 each
Butter	1/2 oz.
Ground white pepper	to taste
Salt	to taste
White wine	1 fl oz.
Chicken Stock	1/4 pt.
Dried bay leaves	1 ea.
Dried ground thyme	1 teaspoon
Dried tarragon	1/4 tsp
All-purpose flour	1/4 oz.
Heavy cream	1 fl oz.
Fresh tarragon (garnish) as needed	

Directions:

1. Trim any fat from the breasts.
2. Select a pan that will just hold the breasts when they are placed close together. Rub the pan with approximately 1/2 ounce butter.
3. Season the chicken breasts with salt and white pepper and arrange them in the buttered pan, presentation side up.
4. Add the wine, stock, bay leaf, thyme and dried tarragon.
5. Cut and butter a piece of parchment paper and cover the chicken breasts.
6. Bring the liquid to a simmer and reduce the temperature to poach the chicken.
7. Make a blond roux with 1-ounce butter and the flour; set aside to cool.
8. When the breasts are done, remove them from the liquid. Thicken the liquid with the roux. Add the cream. Simmer and reduce to the desired consistency.
9. Strain the sauce through cheesecloth and adjust the seasonings.
10. Serve each half breast with approximately 2 fluid ounces sauce; garnish each portion with a sprig of fresh tarragon.

Chicken Satay

Boneless skinless chicken breast	(8 oz.) 1 lb.
Marinade	
Vegetable oil	1 fl oz.
Lemongrass (chopped)	1 tablespoon
Garlic (chopped)	1 tablespoon
Crushed red pepper	1 1/2 tsp
Curry powder	1 1/2 tsp
Honey	1 1/2 tsp
Fish sauce	1 1/2 tsp

Asian-Style Peanut Sauce	
Soy sauce	3 tablespoon
Rice wine vinegar	1 tablespoon
Sugar in the raw	¼ cup
Salt	1 teaspoon
Green onion (minced)	¼ cup
Garlic (minced)	2 cloves
Peanut butter	¾ cup
Hot sauce	to taste

Fresh cilantro (for garnish) as needed
Lime (cut into wedges, for garnish) as needed

Directions:

1. Cut the chicken into 2-ounce strips approximately 4 inches long. Lightly pound the strips with a mallet.
2. Thread the strips onto 6-inch bamboo skewers that have been soaked in water.
3. To make the marinade, combine the marinade ingredients in the bowl of a food processor and puree until smooth.
4. Brush the meat with the marinade and allow to marinate for 1 hour.
5. For peanut sauce combine all ingredients together and puree in a food processor.
6. Grill the skewers until done, approximately 2 minutes. Serve with Southeast Asian–Style Peanut Sauce garnished with cilantro and lime wedges.

Stir-fry Chicken

Chicken Meat, Chopped	2 lbs.
Marinade	
Oil	2 tablespoon
Garlic	1 tablespoon
Ginger	1 tablespoon
Sesame Oil, Pure	1 tablespoon
Cornstarch	2 tablespoon
Soy Sauce	¼ cup
Eggs	2 each

Vegetable Prep

Red Onion, Sliced	1 each
Cashews	½ cup
Bell Pepper, Diced	2 each
Carrots, Julienne	4 each
Celery, Diced	1 cup
Sugar Snap Peas	1 lb.
Sesame Oil	As Needed (To Cook)
Scallion, For Garnish	2 cups

Directions:

1. Trim and cut the chicken into medium-diced pieces.
2. Marinate the chicken with the oil, garlic, ginger, sesame oil, cornstarch, soy sauce, and eggs.
3. Over high heat in a blue steel pan, stir-fry the chicken, in blended sesame oil.
4. Add the onions, peppers, carrots, and celery.
5. Cook until heated through and just tender.
6. Add the sauce.
7. Toss with sliced green onions, sugar snap peas, and cashew nuts.
8. Taste and adjust the seasoning.
9. Serve over Sesame Jasmine Rice.

Chicken Stir-Fry Sauce

Canola oil	¼ cup
Fermented black beans	3 oz.
Garlic, minced	¼ cup
Ginger, minced	1 tablespoon
Soy Sauce	4 oz.
Mirin/Sherry	1 cup
Brown sugar	2 oz.
Chili sauce (Sambal)	1 tablespoon
Water	1 qt.
Cornstarch slurry	as needed, make with Mirin/Sherry

Directions:

1. Soak the fermented black beans in hot water for 10 minutes.
2. Drain and chop the fermented beans.
3. Cook the garlic and black beans in the vegetable oil.
4. Add the remainder of the ingredients and bring to a boil.
5. Simmer for five minutes and thicken with cornstarch slurry.
6. Puree with the immersion blender.

Sautéed down with one (1) cup of stock and then tighten up with cornstarch if needed.

Sautéed Chicken with Curry Sauce

Chicken Breast	
Flour, AP	as needed
Curry	as needed
Salt	as needed
Pepper	as needed

Directions:

1. Pound chicken with a meat mallet on a plastic lined table.
2. Dredge in flour, seasoned with curry, salt and pepper and then sear (you may need to use multiple pans because we will use the pan drippings for your sauce).
3. Remove the chicken from the pan(s).
4. Use these pan(s) to make the sauce.
5. Place the chicken on sheet pan(s) to finish in a 350°F oven.

For The Sauce

Curry Powder	1 Tbsp.
Red Onion, Julienne	½ each
Apples, Small Diced Skin on	1 each
Cider Vinegar	Oz.
Apple Juice	½ cups
Cream	1 cup.
Coconut Milk	¼ cup
Salt	to Taste
Pepper	to Taste

Directions:

1. After the chicken is removed, toast the curry.
2. Add the onions and apples and cook for 2-3 minutes.
3. Deglaze pan with cider vinegar.
4. Add apple juice, and reduce.
5. Add cream, coconut milk, and simmer to develop the flavors.
6. Season with salt and pepper.
7. Thicken with a slurry as needed

Braised Chicken with Mushrooms and Red Wine

Bone in Chicken	5 lbs.
Red Wine (Sweet)	2 cup
Balsamic Vinegar	2 cup
Chicken Stock, Rich	3 quarts
Mushrooms, Sliced	lbs.
Onions, large chop	1 cup
Celery , large chop	½ cup
Carrots, large chop	½ cup
Garlic, Minced	2 cloves
Canola Oil	1 cups
Tomato Paste	1 cups
Parsley	¼ cup
Tarragon	1 tablespoon
Salt and pepper	To Taste

Directions:

1. Season the chicken and sear on all sides using a heavy bottom roaster.
2. Remove the chicken from the pan.
3. Add the mushrooms, onions, celery and carrots
4. Deglaze the pan with the red wine and reduce by 1/2.
5. Add the chicken, garlic, stock, and tomato paste to the pan and bring back to a simmer.
6. Adjust the seasoning of the cooking liquid and finish in a 300°F oven for 1-1 ½ hours or until tender.
7. Remove the chicken and skim the sauce to remove any excess fat.
8. Reduce or slurry the sauce if necessary.
9. Pick the meat off the bones and return to the sauce.
10. Add the parsley and tarragon to finish the sauce and serve.

Apricot and Bourbon Grilled Chicken

Marinade	
Dijon mustard	2 oz
dark brown sugar	2 oz
soy sauce	1 fl oz
bourbon	1 fl oz
worcestershire sauce	1 teaspoon
boneless skinless chicken breast	8 oz 2 ea

Basting sauce	
apricot preserves	2 oz
white wine vinegar	1 fl oz
worcestershire sauce	2 teaspoon
Dijon mustard	2 teaspoon
honey	2 teaspoon
red chile flakes (crushed)	1/4 teaspoon

Vegetables	
onion (sliced into thin rings)	4 oz
all purpose flour	2 oz
salt	to taste
ground black pepper	to taste
zucchini (grilled)	as needed
red bell pepper (grilled)	as needed
yellow squash (grilled)	as needed

Directions

1. Combine the marinade ingredients and transfer to a shallow stainless steel pan.
2. Trim any excess fat from the chicken breasts. Split each breast into two pieces by removing the small piece of cartilage that joins the halves.
3. Place the chicken in the marinade and turn several times to coat it well. Cover the pan with plastic wrap and refrigerate for 1 to 3 hours.
4. Combine the basting sauce ingredients in a small saucepan and simmer for 10 minutes to blend the flavors. Strain if desired and refrigerate until needed.
5. A few minutes before service, place the flour in a shallow pan and season with salt and pepper. Toss the onion rings in the seasoned flour to coat well. Shake off the excess flour and deep fry the rings at 350°F (180°C) until browned.
6. Drain the rings on a paper towel-lined pan and hold in a warm place.

7. Remove the chicken from the marinade, pat dry and place on a preheated grill, presentation side down.
8. Grill for approximately 2 minutes, then brush with the basting sauce. Carefully loosen the chicken from the grill with a spatula, then turn and brush with more basting sauce. Continue to baste frequently and grill until done.
9. Serve with grilled vegetables. Garnish with the fried onion rings at service time.

Chapter 6

LAMB

Marinated Lamb with Yogurt Sauce

Garlic, cloves	4 each
Fresh rosemary (chopped)	3 tablespoons
Oregano (dried)	1 1/2 teaspoons
Kosher salt and freshly ground black pepper	to taste
Freshly squeezed lemon juice	1/2 cup
Olive oil	1/2 cup
Red wine	1/2 cup
Lamb, frenched and cut into 8 chops each	2 racks

Yogurt Mint Sauce:

Scallions, chopped	6 each
Fresh dill (minced)	2 tablespoon
Red pepper flakes	to taste
Olive oil	1 tablespoon
Lemon juice	1 tablespoon
Honey	1 oz.
Greek-style yogurt	7 oz.
Kosher salt	1 teaspoon
Freshly ground black pepper	½ teaspoon

Directions:

1. Place the garlic, rosemary, oregano, 1 1/2 teaspoons salt, and 3/4 teaspoon pepper in the bowl of a food processor and pulse until the herbs are finely minced.
2. Add the lemon juice, olive oil and red wine and combine.
3. Place the chops in a glass or ceramic dish just large enough to hold them in a single layer. Pour the marinade over the chops, turning to coat both sides. Cover with and refrigerate for at least 2 hours but preferably overnight.
4. When ready to cook, prepare a grill to medium-high heat. Remove the lamb from the marinade, sprinkle generously with salt and pepper, and grill for 4 to 5 minutes on each side.
5. Remove to a platter, cover tightly with aluminum foil, and set aside to rest for 10 minutes. Serve hot with the cold Yogurt Sauce.

Yogurt Sauce

1. Place the scallions, dill, red pepper flakes, olive oil, and lemon juice in the bowl of a food processor fitted with the steel blade and puree until it's a coarse paste.

2. Add the yogurt, honey, salt, and pepper and pulse until combined. Transfer to a bowl, cover, and refrigerate for a few hours to allow the flavors to develop.

Honey and Balsamic Lamb Chops

Balsamic vinegar	1/3 cup
Garlic	1 clove
Honey	2 tablespoon
Canola oil	¾ cup
Kosher salt and freshly ground black pepper	to toast
Lamb chops (small)	8 each
Olive oil	2 tablespoon
Fresh rosemary (chopped)	1 tablespoon

Directions:

1. Place a grill pan over medium-high heat or preheat a gas or charcoal grill.
2. In the bowl of a food processor, combine the balsamic vinegar, garlic, and honey. Pulse until blended. With the machine running, slowly pour in the vegetable oil until the mixture is smooth and forms a thick sauce. Season with salt and pepper, to taste.
3. Season the lamb chops with salt and pepper. Drizzle with the olive oil and sprinkle with rosemary. Grill the lamb chops for 2 to 3 minutes each side until medium-rare.
4. Arrange the lamb chops on a platter. Spoon the sauce over the top or serve the sauce on the side.

Lamb Kabobs

Lamb	1 lbs. (from shoulder or leg)
Salt and Pepper	To Taste
Mushroom, Button (remove steams)	10 each (cut in half)
Green Bell Pepper	1 ½ each
Red Onion	1 each
Tomatoes, Grape	½ lb.
Pineapple, Diced	½ each
Marinade:	
Mint	½ cup
Thyme	½ cup
Oil	½ cup
Sherry	½ cup
Metal Skewers	8-10 each

Directions:

1. Trim the lamb and cut into 1 to ½ inch cubes.
2. Cut the mushrooms in half.
3. Cut the bell pepper and onion into 1-inch flat pieces.
4. Wash the grape tomatoes
5. Season the lamb with salt and pepper.
6. Skewer the lamb, pepper, onion, mushrooms, tomatoes, and pineapple onto the metal skewers.
7. Combine the ingredients for the marinade.
8. Marinate the skewers.
9. Grill and brush with the excess marinade.
10. Finish in the oven, cooking to medium.

Roasted Lamb Rack

Lamb Rack	4 each
Salt and Pepper	To Taste
Dijon Mustard	½ cup
Bread Crumbs, Fresh	1 cup
Herbs, fresh	¼ cup

Directions:

1. Season and sear the lamb.
2. Brush with Dijon mustard. Coat with Herbed breadcrumbs.
3. Roast to and internal temperature of 130°F in a 300°F oven. (About 20-30 minutes).

Curried Lamb Stew

Lamb Shoulder	3-4 lbs.
Sesame Oil	2 tablespoon
Salt	to Taste
Chiles, Flakes	1 tablespoon
Coriander Seed	1 ½ tablespoon
Mustard Seed	1 ½ tablespoon
Cumin	1 teaspoon
Fenugreek	1 teaspoon
Vegetable Oil	6 tablespoon
Onion, Sliced	3 each
Garlic, Crushed	4 cloves
Lemon Juice	1 lemon
Tamarind	1 ½ teaspoon
Asafetida	1 teaspoon
Brown Sugar	1 tablespoon
Veal Stock	2 cups
Cilantro	¼ cup
Scallion	¼ cup

Directions:

1. Trim the lamb meat from all fat and connective tissue.
2. Cut the lamb into 1-inch pieces and season with salt and sesame oil.
3. Set aside.
4. Grind the chili flakes, coriander, mustard, cumin, and fenugreek in a spice grinder.
5. Place the spices in a pan under medium heat with the vegetable oil and cook until they become aromatic and brown.
6. Add the lamb and brown on all sides.
7. Remove from the pan.
8. Add the onion and garlic and sweat so that they release their flavor and breakdown.
9. Add the reserved lamb, lemon juice, tamarind, asafetida, brown sugar, and veal stock.
10. Bring to a simmer and adjust the flavor with additional salt as necessary.
11. Place a tight fitting lid on the pot and put in a 250° oven for about 1 hour or until tender and falling apart.
12. Once tender adjust the flavor of the lamb and finish with the cilantro, scallions, and serve with rice or lentils.

Chapter 7

Vegetarian, Vegan Salads and Dishes

Couscous Salad

Olive Oil	1 Tbsp.
Couscous Regular	10 oz.
Stock	1 cups
Salt	¼ tsp.

Garnish:

Red Bell Pepper – Small Dice	½ each
Green Bell Pepper – Small Dice	½ each
Green Onions – Sliced On the Bias	½ bunch
Cucumbers – Peeled, Seeded, Small Dice	½ each
Black Olives – Pitted and Sliced	2 oz.
Red Onion – Small Dice	3 oz.

Dressing:

Orange Juice and Zest, of	2 each
Rice Vinegar	2 oz.
Garlic, Chopped	1 tsp.
Salt	1 tsp.
Pepper	1 tsp.
Fresh Oregano, Chopped	2 tsp.
Salad Oil	3 oz.
Honey	1 oz.
Fresh Thyme, Chopped	2 tsp.

Directions:

1. Bring the stock to a boil and add the salt, oil and couscous.
2. Cover and remove from the heat.
3. Let stand covered for 5 minutes.
4. Fluff and combine the couscous with the vegetables.
5. Whisk together all of the dressing ingredients.
6. Combine the salad ingredients with the dressing.
7. Chill thoroughly before serving.

Vegetarian Pad Thai

Rice Noodles	1 lbs.
Tofu, Firm, Diced/Sliced	½ lbs.
Sesame Oil Blend	¼ cup
Cashew Nuts	¼ cup
Raisins	as needed
Spring Onions	10 each
Bean Sprouts	2 oz.

Directions:

1. Soak the rice noodles in hot water for about 10-12 minutes.
2. Drain and reserve.
3. Divide your ingredients into 1/3 (each will make a batch).
4. Sauté the tofu and cashew nuts.
5. Add the rice noodles and stir-fry for about 1 minute.
6. Add the sauce (1/3).
7. Add the raisins, spring onions, and bean sprouts.
8. Cook until the sprouts become tender.
9. Pan up and garnish with peanuts, cilantro, and fresh bean sprouts.
10. Serve with lime wedges on the side.

SAUCE:

Soy Sauce	½ cup
Sugar	½ cup
Lemon Juice	½ cup
Peanut Butter	3 oz.
Pineapple	1 ½ oz.
Sugar, Brown	2 oz.
Vinegar	½ Tbsp.
Salt	as needed
Ketchup	¼ cup
Stock, Vegetable	¼ cup

Directions:

11. Combine all of this together and puree.
12. Reserve the sauce for assembly of the dish.

GARNISH

Chopped Peanuts, Cilantro, Lime and Bean Sprouts

Polenta

Cornmeal	2 cups.
Water (may substitute milk)	5 cups
Butter	½ Tbsp.
Salt and Pepper	To Taste
Flavorings	as needed

Directions:

1. Heat the water and butter with flavorings and salt and pepper.
2. Once the liquid has come to a boil, remove from heat and slowly add the cornmeal while whisking the liquid vigorously!
3. Return to heat and bring to a boil.
4. The polenta can be further cooked in the oven with a lid. This will yield soft polenta.

Flavor Ideas for Polenta

1. Garlic, Rosemary, and Parmesan
2. Lemon Zest and Rosemary
3. Garlic and Sautéed Mushrooms
4. Fresh Herbs

Quinoa

Onions, Small Dice	1 cup
Carrot, Small Dice	½ cup
Celery, Small Dice	½ cup
Canola Oil	4 Tbsp.
Quinoa	2 cups
Chicken Stock	1 qt.
Kosher Salt	To Taste
Pepper	To Taste
Butter	2 oz.

Directions:

1. Rinse the quinoa. (This helps to make quinoa less sticky).
2. In a saucepot, sauté the onions, carrot, and celery in the canola oil over medium heat.
3. Add the quinoa and allow it to brown slightly.
4. Add the stock and season with salt and pepper.
5. Bring to a full simmer.
6. Reduce the heat and simmer for 3-5 minutes.
7. Remove from the stove and cover the pot.
8. Allow the quinoa to steep until tender, approximately 8 minutes.
9. Finish with the butter, and serve immediately, hot.

Roasted Vegetable with Couscous
(For Animah Talawahe)

For Roasted Vegetables

Green peppers, sliced	½ each
Cauliflower florets	½ cup
Fingerling potatoes, halved	4-5 each
carrots, large dice	2 each
red onion, large dice	½ each
olive oil	as needed
salt and pepper	as needed
sunflower seeds	garnish
bean sprouts	garnish

Directions:

1. Preheat oven to 450.
2. Place peppers, cauliflower, potatoes, carrots and onions on a sheet pan. Drizzle with olive oil and season with salt and pepper.
3. Roasted for approximately 30-35 minutes or until all vegetables are tender and caramelized.

For Couscous

olive Oil	1 Tbsp.
couscous, regular	10 oz.
Vegetable stock	1 cups
salt	¼ tsp.

1. Bring the stock to a boil and add the salt, oil and couscous.
2. Cover and remove from the heat.
3. Let stand covered for 5 minutes.
4. Fluff and combine the couscous with the vegetables.

Yellow Rice Salad with Roasted Peppers and Spicy Black Beans

Ground cumin	4 tsp.
fresh lime juice	¼ cup
vegetable oil	2 ½ Tbsp.
turmeric	½ tsp.
Water	2 cups
basmati rice	1 cup
Salt	1 tsp.
red onions, thinly sliced	½ cup
can black beans, rinsed, drained	16 oz.
roasted red peppers, chopped	½ cup
green bell pepper, chopped	½ cup
fresh cilantro, chopped	1/3 cup
chipotle chiles, minced	1 ½ tsp.

Directions:

1. To create a dressing, Stir 3 teaspoons cumin in small dry skillet over medium heat just until fragrant, about 1 minute. Remove from heat. Whisk limejuice and oil into skillet. Stir turmeric and remaining cumin in heavy medium saucepan over medium heat until fragrant, about 1 minute.
2. Add 2 cups water, rice and salt; bring to boil. Reduce heat to low and cover; simmer until water is absorbed, about 15 minutes. Cool rice. Mix onions and half of dressing into rice. Season with salt and pepper.
3. Combine black beans, all peppers, cilantro, chipotle chilies, and remaining dressing in medium bowl. Toss to coat. Season with salt and pepper.
4. Mound bean mixture in center of platter. Surround with rice salad.

Green tacos

Olive oil	3 Tbsp.
sweet potato, peeled, grated	1 each (small)
garlic , finely chopped	1 clove
kale, ribs and stems removed, torn into bite-size pieces	4 cups
lime juice	2 Tbsp..
Kosher salt, freshly ground pepper	as needed
corn tortillas, warmed	4 each
avocado, thinly sliced	1 each
crema mexicana	¼ cup

Directions:

1. Heat oil in a medium saucepan over medium heat. Cook sweet potato and garlic, stirring often, until potato is tender and just beginning to brown, 8–10 minutes. Add kale and cook, tossing often, until kale is wilted and tender, 8–10 minutes. Add limejuice and season with salt and pepper.
2. Serve sweet potato and kale mixture on tortillas, topped with avocado and crema mexicana

Spinach Salad with Crispy Shallots and Dates

Dates, pitted	2 each
additional dates, chopped	¾ cup
finely grated lime zest	1 tsp.
lime juice	¼ cup
vegetable oil, divided	⅔cup
Kosher salt and freshly ground black pepper	as needed
shallots, thinly sliced	4 each
flat-leaf spinach, trimmed	1 bunch

Directions:

1. Blend whole dates, lime zest, limejuice, and ⅓ cup oil in a blender until smooth; season with salt and pepper.
2. Heat remaining ⅓ cup oil in a medium saucepan over medium-high heat and cook shallots, stirring often, until golden brown and crisp, 5–7 minutes; drain on paper towels and season with salt.
3. Toss spinach and chopped dates with dressing. Top with fried shallots.

Corn and Zucchini Salad

Corn, fresh	4 ears
Kosher salt	as needed
zucchini (small), thinly sliced lengthwise	4 each
fresh basil, coarsely chopped	¼ cup
fresh flat-leaf parsley, coarsely chopped	cup
olive oil	⅓ cup
white wine vinegar	¼ cup
crushed red pepper flakes	½ tsp.
Freshly ground black pepper	as needed
feta, crumbled	Oz.

Directions:

1. Cook corn in a large pot of boiling salted water until bright yellow and tender, about 3 minutes; transfer to a plate and let cool.
2. Cut kernels from cobs and place in a large bowl. Add zucchini, basil, parsley, oil, vinegar, and red pepper flakes and toss to combine; season with salt and pepper. Serve topped with feta.

Arugula, Red Onion and Pomegranate Salads

Red onion, thinly sliced	1 large
sugar	1½ tsp.
ground sumac	1 tsp.
(available at specialty food stores)	
Kosher salt	as needed
olive oil	3 Tbsp.
red wine vinegar	1 Tbsp.
honey	½ tsp.
Arugulas	4 cups
pomegranate seeds	¼ cup

Directions:

1. Toss onion, sugar, and sumac in a medium bowl; season with salt and let sit 30 minutes. Add oil, vinegar, and honey and toss to combine; let sit 5 minutes.
2. Just before serving, toss in arugula and pomegranate seeds; season with salt.

Israeli Couscous with Saffron and Spring Vegetables

Israeli couscous,dry	2 cups
canola oil	4 tsp.
fennel, slivered, grated, or finely chopped	1 cup
leek, white and pale green parts finely chopped	½ cup
garlic, chopped	6 cloves
dry white wine	½ cup
Peas (shelled fresh or frozen)	2 cups
vegetable broth	1 cup
plum tomatoes, chopped	1 cup
saffron threads	2-3 strands
baby arugula leaves	2 cups
olive oil	3 Tbsp.
Fresh basil leaves	garnish

Directions:

1. Prepare couscous according to package directions. Set aside.
2. Heat canola oil in large skillet over medium-high heat. Add fennel, leek, and garlic, and cook 3 to 5 minutes, or until lightly browned.
3. Stir in wine, and cook 1 minute to deglaze pan. Add peas, and let wine reduce 1 minute more, then add broth. Add couscous, tomatoes, and saffron; season with salt and pepper, if desired. Cover, and let stand 5 minutes. Stir in arugula, and remove from heat. Season with salt and pepper, if desired.
4. Spoon into bowls, then top with olive oil and basil.

Endive, Pear & Walnut Salad with Raspberry Vinaigrette

Raspberry Vinaigrette

Raspberry vinegar	2 Tbsp.
Honey	1 Tbsp.
Dijon mustard	1 tsp.
flaxseed oil	2 tsp.
extra virgin olive oil	1 ½ Tbsp.
Water	1 Tbsp.
kosher salt	¼ tsp.
freshly ground pepper	⅛ tsp.

Salad

4 medium-sized heads red Belgian endive, leaves separated and cut into 1-inch pieces
1 bunch watercress, rinsed and torn into small pieces
1 large Asian pear, peeled, cored and thinly sliced
2 oz. chopped walnuts, toasted

Directions:

1. To make Raspberry Vinaigrette: Whisk together vinegar, honey and mustard in bowl. Slowly whisk in oils and water until emulsified. Season with salt and pepper. Set aside.
2. To make Endive, Pear & Walnut Salad: Toss endive and watercress in salad bowl. Re-whisk vinaigrette just before serving; pour over salad greens, tossing to coat. Divide salad among 6 serving plates. Top each with pears and walnuts.

Vegan Chili

onion, chopped	2 cups
garlic, minced	3 cloves
chipotle chile in adobo sauce, drained and minced	1 each
baby bella mushrooms, finely chopped	1 ½ cups
seitan, chopped	3 cups
tomato paste	3 Tbsp.
smoked paprika	2 tsp.
dried oregano	2 tsp.
chili powder	1 ½ tsp.
celery salt	¾ tsp.
chili beans, canned, partially drained	(3) 15-oz. cans
carrots, chopped	1 cup
low-sodium tamari or soy sauce	2 Tbsp.
Worcestershire sauce	1 Tbsp.

Directions:

1. Heat oil in Dutch oven over medium-high heat. Add onion, and sauté 7 to 10 minutes, or until beginning to brown, stirring often. Add garlic and chipotle chile, and sauté 1 minute more. Stir in mushrooms; cook 3 to 4 minutes, or until softened. Add seitan, tomato paste, paprika, oregano, chili powder, celery salt, and 1-cup water; cook 3 to 4 minutes, stirring occasionally.
2. Add beans, carrots, tamari, and Worcestershire sauce. Cover, and reduce heat to medium-low. Simmer 1 hour, or until carrots are tender.

Vegan Paella

Olive oil	2 Tbs.
spicy marinated tofu, finely diced	(2) 7-oz. pkgs.
cremini mushrooms, sliced	8 oz.
carrots, diced	1 cup
corn kernels, fresh or frozen	2 cups
chopped tomatoes, drained	14 oz.
garlic, minced	4 cloves
short-grain brown rice	1 cup
saffron, crumbled	⅛ tsp.
Peas, fresh or frozen, thawed	1 cup
lemon juice	¼ cup
green onions, thinly sliced,	for garnish

Directions:

1. Heat oil in wok over medium-high heat. Add tofu when ripples appear in oil, and season with salt. Sauté 10 minutes, or until tofu is browned, stirring occasionally. Add mushrooms, and sauté 4 to 5 minutes, or until mushrooms release liquid and begin to brown.
2. Stir in carrots, corn, tomatoes, and garlic, and sauté 2 minutes more. Stir in rice, 2 1/4 cups water, and saffron. Bring paella to a boil. Reduce heat to medium-low, cover with wok lid, and simmer 40 minutes, or until all liquid is absorbed. Add peas on surface (do not stir yet), cover, and allow peas to steam 1 to 2 minutes. Remove wok from heat, and stir in lemon juice and green onions. Season with salt and pepper.

Spicy Orange Slaw

Carrots, grated	2 cups
purple cabbage, shredded	2 cups
chopped cilantro	½ cup
roasted pumpkin seeds	¼ cup
frozen orange juice concentrate, thawed	3 Tbsp.
fresh lime juice	1 Tbsp.
ground cumin	½ tsp.
cayenne pepper	¼ tsp.
kosher salt	¼ tsp.

Directions:

Combine all ingredients in medium bowl, and toss well to mix.

Chapter 8

Fly Ty's Fruit Smoothies and Juices

Fruit Smoothies

This is something simple and quick for when you just want to get up and go.

R.B.G Banana Blast

Bananas	2 to 3
Strawberries	5 to 6
Blueberries	1/3 cup
Protein Powder	Of your choice
Almond Milk	As Needed
Honey	To Taste

***Note Almond milk can be replace with Hemp or Rice milk**
***All recipes are measured for one serving**

Asatta Avocado Blend

Avocados	1
Bananas	3
Strawberries	5 to 6
Pineapples	1/3 cup diced up
Flax Seeds	As Needed
Almond Milk	As Needed
Protein Powder	Of Choice

All recipes are measured for one serving

Avocados ar full of "good fats, which can lower bad cholesterol levels. They are thick and creamy and are great for thickening your

Blueberry Banger

lueberries re full of Antioxidants, Vhich boost our immune ystem and revent nfections.

Blueberries	½ cup
Pears	½
Strawberries	5 to 6
Bananas	3
Pineapple	1/3 cup
Protein Powder	Of Choice
Flax Seed Oil	As recommended
Raw Honey	As Needed
Almond Milk	As Needed

All recipes are measured for one serving

Amazing Apple

Apples (Green or Red)	1
Strawberries	1/3 cup
Banana	3
Flax Seeds (Or oil)	As Needed
Wheat Germ	As Needed
Protein Powder	Of Choice
Almond Milk	As Needed

***All recipes are measured for one serving**

The pectin in apples is known to lower the body's need for insulin and may help in diabetes management

Peanut Butter Bonanza

I usually carry this blend with me for lunch to go with my meal.

Peanut Butter Tablespoons	4
Organic oats	½ cup
Bananas	3
Wheat Germ	As Needed
Raw Honey	As Needed
Flax Seeds	As Needed
Almond Milk	As Needed
Protein Powder	Of Choice

All recipes are measured for one serving

Perfectly Pineapple

Pineapples	½ Cup Diced
Strawberries	½ Cup
Pears	1
Bananas	2
Raw Honey	As Needed
Flax seed Oil	As Needed
Almond Milk	As Needed

All recipes are measured for one serving

The Vitamin C in pineapples may help lower your risk for heart disease, gout, cancer, lead toxicity, cataracts and stroke.

Fly Boy's Fave

normally have his in the norning if I on't feel like naking reakfast. It's uick, easy and lling 'til your ext meal.

Bananas	3
Avocados	1
Blueberries	1/3 cup
Apples	1
Pears	1
Strawberries	5 to 6
Cashews	Hand full
Flax Seeds	As Needed
Wheat Germ	As Needed
Almond Milk	As Needed
Protein powder	Of Choice

All recipes are measured for one serving

Mucho Mango

Mangos	½ diced up
Bananas	2 to 3
Raw honey	2 tbsp.
Almond milk	As Needed
Protein Powder	Of Choice
Flax Seeds	As Needed

Add Ice Cubes If Needed

All recipes are measured for one serving

Potassium in Mangos is known to reduce higher blood pressure levels.

ipe papaya s a eneficial ource of ntioxidant itamin C, itamin E nd arotenoids ke beta-arotene and copene.

Potent Papaya

Papaya	1/3 Diced
Strawberries	1/3 Cup
Avocado	1
Almond milk	As Needed
Raw Honey	As Needed
Flax Seed Oil	As Recommended

All recipes are measured for one serving

Banana Berry

Bananas	3
Blueberries	½ cup
Raw Honey	As Needed
Protein Powder	As Needed
Flax Seed Oil	As Needed
Almond Milk	As Needed

All recipes are measured for one serving

The B6 in bananas acts as an anti-inflammatory agent.

Fruit/Vegetable Juices

Citrus Punch

Lemons	1
Oranges	2
Pineapples	1/3 cup diced
Orange Juice	3 cups
Ice cubes	As Needed
Ginger	1 Nice Piece

Not recommended for people with Acid Reflux
Be sure not to use too much Ginger as it may make it too strong

Ginger Detox

Ginger	I Nice Size Piece
Carrots	8 to 10
Apple	2
Lemons	1

Be sure not to use too much Ginger as it may make it too strong

You Can't Beet It

Beets	1 Large
Apples	2
Ginger	1 Nice Piece
Carrots	8 to 10

***Be sure not to use too much Ginger as it may make it too strong**

Love my Lemons

Lemon juice	1/3 cup
Lemons	2
Pineapple	1/3 diced cup
Oranges	2
Orange juice	3 cups
Ice Cubes	As Needed

Green Beret

Kale	1 Bunch
Aloe Vera	Half Leaf
Celery	1 Bunch
Cucumbers	2
Spinach	1 Bunch
Parsley	1 Bunch

***Wheatgrass if available**
***Green Protein Powder**

Verrry Veggie

Broccoli	1 Bunch
Kale	1 Bunch
Spinach	1 Bunch
Celery	1 Bunch
Cucumbers	3
Watercress	1 Bunch
Parsley	1 Bunch
Garlic	1/3 clove

***Wheatgrass if available**
*** Green Protein Powder**

Alkaline Me

Celery	1 Bunch
Aloe Vera	½ Leaf
Cucumbers	3
Watercress	1 Bunch
Alkaline Water	As Needed
Lemon juice	1/3 Cup

Sweet Greens

Kale	1 Bunch
Spinach	1 Bunch
Celery	1 Bunch
Cucumbers	2
Pineapples	1/3 Cup Diced
Green Apples	2
Broccoli	1 Bunch

**** Green Protein Powder***

Cucumber Quicky

Cucumbers	3
Celery	1 Bunch
Pineapple	1/3 diced cup
Green Apple	1

The End

Be sure to check out my other publications:

-Flyboys Book of Poetry Volume 1

-Flyboys Book of Poetry Volume 2

-Intimate Thoughts of an Original Man
(Flyboys Book of Poetry Volume 3)

-Destiny's First Day – A look at African
American Hair Issues (Short Story)

-My Thoughts in Rhyme – (The Facts of Life in
The Ghetto R.B.G Edition Volume 1)

-A Message to Our Suns
(Listen up Young Man)

-Fly Ty Unchained Presents:
(Letters from the Diaspora) Featuring Various Writers

-Locs, Life and Love Pt 1 The Knotty Chroniclez
(Written By: Andre'a Deberry & Fly Ty Unchained

-Locs, Life and Love Pt 2 The Knotty Chroniclez
(Written By: Andre'a Deberry & Fly Ty Unchained

All available on:
Lulu.com/spotlight/FlyboyTy

You can also contact me at:
madeintheimageofgod@yahoo.com

FLY TY UNCHAINED 2014

www.ingramcontent.com/pod-product-compliance
Ingram Content Group UK Ltd.
Pitfield, Milton Keynes, MK11 3LW, UK
UKHW041941190726
13854UKWH00004B/1726